ATTENTION TO DETAIL

A GENTLEMAN'S GUIDE TO PROFESSIONAL APPEARANCE AND CONDUCT

CLINTON T. GREENLEAF III

D1548676

DEDICATION

This book is dedicated to my grandparents,
Julie, Alex, Millie and Clint.
Thank you for your love, guidance and support. I love you.

©1998 by Clinton Tuxberry Greenleaf III

Illustrations by Danielle Khas

Layout by Francine

Edited by Holly Strawbridge

Assistants: Helen and Geof Greenleaf, Jennifer Sheehan, Helen Knipe,
Beth Reardon, Wilma Maples, Mark Chockley and Lee Arthurs

Published in the United States by Greenleaf Enterprises, Cleveland, Ohio.

1998 Second Edition

TABLE OF CONTENTS

INTRODUCTION

Let's face it: in today's world, appearance and conduct matter. People are initially judged by the way they look. They earn their credibility based on how they act. Those who want to succeed take the time to look their best and act appropriately on all occasions.

No matter your background, you can learn to look great and conduct yourself like a professional by reading this book. You will learn that attention to detail matters, not only in your career, but in all aspects of your life. The level of care reflected in your appearance and manners attracts positive attention and admiration, which fosters confidence. Most importantly, you will begin to pay more attention to detail – a skill highly valued in the professional world.

---|**1**|---

Why Appearance Matters

Who ever decided that tying some fabric around your neck will make you look more serious, or wearing shoes that are shined will give you the appearance of a go-getter? Research studies show that there is a high correlation between appearance and perceptions of professional abilities. Also, your first impression is the one that remains in most people's eyes.

But the derivation and theories of societal grooming standards are not the point of this book, so it will not delve deeply into the realm of why it matters. As a reader, simply accept that it does. This book takes the stance that although individualism and self-expressionism are important, for most of us, dressing appropriately for the professional environment is necessary for success. For those of you who wish to compete in today's professional world, this book is for you. While being well dressed is not enough alone to ensure success, an unprofessional appearance will almost guarantee failure. The point is not to tell you what you must do or wear, but to guide you in what is acceptable and preferred today. Even if you choose not to follow any of the suggestions, you will learn what it takes to display a professional image.

Shoes

Let us start with shoes. A great shine on your shoes can really enhance your professional image. The trick to a sparkling shoe shine is not of elbow grease, but technique. Once you have learned it, your shoes will stay shined all day, and your overall appearance will be noticeably improved.

First, buy some shoe polish; you can find it at any drug or grocery store. Also, be sure the polish matches your shoe color. Use black on black shoes, brown on brown shoes and cordovan on maroon shoes.

Place a few old newspapers on the floor before you start. You'll also need a cotton rag (an old T-shirt will do) a bit of water, and about 30 minutes per shoe. Separate each shoe into seven sections: (1) toe, (2) right front, (3) right back, (4) the heel, (5) left back, (6) left front and (7) tongue. Work on only one section at a time. Open your polish

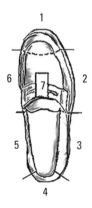

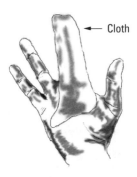

Cloth

tin and fill the top cover with lukewarm water. Take your cloth rag and wrap it tightly around your right index and middle fingers.

Polish Motion

Touch your fingers to the water in the lid, then smack them against your left palm to make sure the cloth is not too wet. Make a few circles in the polish with the moist rag. Now, using light pressure, make circles of polish on the first section of the shoe. The trick here is to make small, tight circles as your fingers move around the section in a circular motion. As you apply the polish to your shoe, it will blur any existing shine. This means the polish is filling every pore in the leather. By moving in circles, you will compact the polish in each pore. Once all pores are filled with polish, a shine will become visible as light is reflected off the smooth, flat surface.

Once you have applied polish to the first section, move your fingers to a clean part of the rag. Wet it as described above. Using water only, make the same polishing motion with a little less pressure on the same section of the shoe. You should notice the beginning of a nice shine. This buffing action will further compact the polish and smooth it

Side

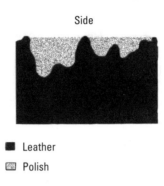

■ Leather
▨ Polish

into the pores of the leather. When you polish each shoe for the first time, repeat the process (starting with new polish, and then buffing it in) three times per section. Once a week, re-shine each section once. This will take only about ten minutes, and will keep your shoes looking great.

Another way to make your shoes look their best is to use edge dressing. This is basically a paint, or dye, that coats the side of the sole. It seals and protects, as well as provides a finished look to your shoes. Several types are available, but Kiwi Honor Guard Edge Dressing is the best. Be careful with edge dressing, though, since it is a permanent dye and stains very easily. Remember to put newspaper on the floor, and apply the dressing only to the outer walls of the soles, not on the bottom. Be sure not to touch the leather, since it is a permanent dye and stains easily. To fill the area where the leather meets the sole, use a cotton swab to apply the edge

Edge Dressing

dressing. Once a week, touch up any areas that may have become scuffed, such as the toe and heel.

After three or four months of constant wear and regular polishing, your shoes will become more difficult to shine. The polish will begin to build up in some areas and to crack and fall off. This leaves uneven layers of polish and a dull shine. To remedy this, you will need to break down the finish. This is a relatively simple but messy process, so, again, lay down some newspaper. You will also need a few rags, a toothbrush and a can of shaving cream, preferably the gel type.

First remove any laces from your shoes so they do not interfere with the process. If you have a gel type cream, spray it on your hand and make sure to work up a good lather. Rub it gently into the leather covering it completely. After both shoes are covered with shaving cream, set them aside for about four hours to break down the chemical bonds of the polish and allow it to detach from the leather. At the same time, the cream will condition the shoe as it moisturizes and softens the leather. After four hours have passed, take your rags and carefully wipe the cream off the shoes. You will notice that along with the cream, your rags will collect some old polish. Be sure to wipe the shaving cream off completely; if it stays on the shoe, it will flake off after you have repolished, and ruin the shine. Use the toothbrush to clean the shaving cream out of the small creases in the leather, and the area where the sole meets the leather.

You should notice after breaking down the finish that the leather is more supple and has a duller shine. This is actually a good process for the shoe and can extend its useful life by as much as 50 percent. Repeat the process of shining as described in the beginning of this chapter.

You will also discover that your shoes will last two to three times longer than usual if you buy at least two pairs, and alternate them daily. For example, if you have a black

Monday Tuesday Wednesday Thursday Friday

and brown pair, you would wear the black on Monday, brown on Tuesday, black on Wednesday, etc. When not being worn, cedar shoe-trees will help them keep their form and allow them to dry and air out completely.

If you are in a professional office environment, be sure to buy leather-soled shoes. Leather soled shoes have a certain quality about them that rubber-soled shoes do not have. The marginal improvement in comfort you see with rubber soles will not replace the loss of credibility you will incur by wearing rubber soles. A good shine and a well-cared-for pair of leather-soled shoes will clearly illustrate your attention to detail and professionalism.

3

SHIRTS

Much of the feedback from the first edition involved questions about the merits of purchasing custom made shirts versus ready made shirts. Essentially, off-the-rack shirts are fine if they fit you well. If your frame is unique, and you find it difficult to find shirts that fit, custom shirts may be for you. Some men consider custom-made shirts superior, but the great majority wear off-the-rack clothes and still look professional.

Although casual Fridays allow us to relax our style of dress once a week, chances are you need to wear a dress shirt to work most of the time. A pressed dress shirt shows that you care about your appearance and helps you look more fit. Have your shirts professionally washed and ironed. It may seem like an unnecessary expense, but the benefits are worth it. For less than two dollars a day, your shirts will be ironed properly. If you check around, you may find dry cleaners who will pick-up and deliver directly to your door.

Front

Pull   Hold   Pull

Back

Fold

A properly pressed shirt must be tucked in well. After you button it, gently pull down and out on the front of the shirt. This will straighten the button line so it is directly in the middle of your body. Now, slide your hands around your sides from your front to your back to bunch any loose cloth in the back. Take the excess in you hands and fold it over towards the outside. Holding your shirt in position, pull up your pants and lock the shirt in place. This trick will keep your front free of wrinkles and folds, and the fold in the back will nicely hide any excess fabric. When you buy your

Excess Fabric   Excess Fabric

shirts, be sure that the material is opaque. It is not appropriate to see chest hair or a T-shirt through the fabric. Also, wear only long-sleeved shirts with a suit. If you feel the need to have shorter sleeves, you can always roll them up.

A T-shirt should be worn underneath most dress shirts even in the summer. The T-shirt should have a full neck and short sleeves. V-necks and tank-tops are visible under most dress shirts and look inappropriate. Wearing a T-shirt is a little warmer, but deal with the heat and cover yourself; it does matter.

Many shirts have colored collars and cuffs made from contrasting color, for example a blue shirt with white collar and cuffs. These shirts come in and out of style and are ac-

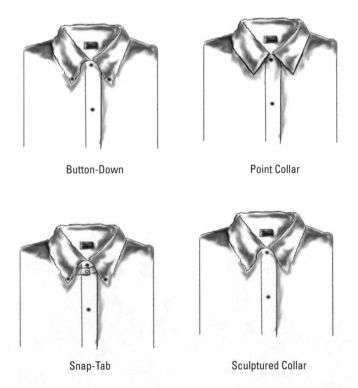

Button-Down   Point Collar

Snap-Tab   Sculptured Collar

ceptable only in certain circles. A good rule is to watch what other people in your office wear, and how certain styles are received. If your office is stylish, feel free to wear such a shirt. If your office is very conservative, you may wish to keep your shirts a solid color. By keeping an eye on the pulse of the office, you show you are paying attention to detail and enhancing your professional appearance.

Several types of shirt collars are available. The picture on the previous page illustrates the four basic types: the button-down collar, the point collar, the snap-tab collar, the sculptured collar. Each type is considered appropriate for business. The right choice depends on personal taste. One word of caution though: if you wear button-down collars, make sure that both sides are buttoned. If your collars are not buttoned down, use collar-stays, small clasps that keep your collar from curling up and looking unprofessional. Remember that your image is always under scrutiny.

Ties

Almost every professional man must wear a tie. Unfortunately, 80 percent look sloppy. This is often the result of a half-Windsor knot, which makes ties appear asymmetrical. A poll of executives revealed that most believe a half-Windsor knot looks unprofessional, and a double-Windsor looks too bulky. The survey concluded that a full-Windsor looks best for business.

Half   Double   Full

To tie a full-Windsor knot, put your tie around your neck with the wide base on the left and the thin end on the right. Pull the tie so that the bottom of the thin section is even with the third button down from the top of your shirt. Now pull the wide section over the thin section, making an

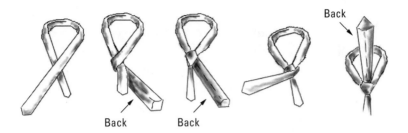

Back

Back   Back

X. With your left hand, reach under the X and pull the wide section under, then over the upper left part of the X. Pull the wide section through the upper half of the X, then through, and then over the left side. Pull the entire wide section left across the X, and up through the back side of the upper half of the X.

Make sure to leave a bit of slack on the front as you pull the wide section through the cross you just made. The wide part should be longer than the thin part, and the tip of the wide part should be even with the bottom of your belt buckle. Be sure that the bottom of the tie does not end above your buckle or extend too far below the belt.

Although prevalent up to and through the 1960s, tie clips and tie pins are no longer in style. If your tie is properly tied, it will remain in place without a clip or pin. But feel free to wear one with your suit, understanding that it conveys an older image.

Most men only wear bow ties with tuxedos, but learning how to tie a bow tie is considered an art. To explain the art of tying a bow tie, assume the following example: the tie we will use is half white, half black, as seen in diagram (1). Begin by wrapping the white end around the middle of the black side, and pull the ends out to the side, much like the first step of tying a shoe (2). Now take the white end, and fold it three ways as seen in the diagram (3). This will form the front of the bow, and a sort of "T". Now press the white bow against your throat, and wrap the black piece over the front, middle, of the tie (4). Make the same kind of three fold "T" with the end of the black piece. Now, pull the black

1

2

3

4

5

6

bow behind the white bow, and between the fabric closest to your neck and the white bow (5). You should end up with two bows, the white in front, and the black in back (6). Now pull gently on the bows to tighten the knot.

Although you may not have many opportunities to wear one, the ability to tie a real bow tie will add credibility to your character. Few men know how. While bow ties are not recommended for daily wear, some professionals make it their style. Professionally speaking, however, bow ties are definitely not mainstream, and possibly the mark of an eccentric.

Pants

Wearing pants seems easy enough, right? While pants are not nearly as problematic as ties or shirts, pants do require a bit of care. In the professional world, you will spend most of your time sitting, which causes your pants to wear faster than your jacket. This will create a mismatch in color and quality between your jacket and pants, which looks quite unprofessional. Although it is somewhat inevitable, there are steps you can take to slow the process.

Carry your wallet in the breast pocket of your jacket instead of your pants to prevent your pant pocket from wearing out. Another option is to carry a money clip for your bills and a card holder for your credit cards and driver's license. If you put one in each front pant pocket, you will be able to carry your valuables with you without seriously damaging your pockets.

Keys and coins are another pocket killer. If you must carry keys, limit them to only the ones you must have to make it through the work day. Both keys and coins will leave outlines on your pants or make holes in your pockets if they are carried in the same pocket day after day. It is considered unprofessional to walk with coins and keys "clinking" around in your pocket, so limit the amount of coins you have and keep them in a different pocket than your keys.

When you remove your suit after the work day is over, folding your pants properly will ensure a good crease and fewer wrinkles. Begin by holding your pants upside down and lining up all four seams. Now pull the front and back of the pant out at the cuff, keeping the seams together. The fold should fall on the natural crease of the pants. Slip the pants onto a hanger, replace the jacket, and hang it up in your closet.

When wrinkles become noticeable, pressing your pants becomes an important part of keeping a professional appearance. Pressed pants will make your suit look sharper and illustrate your attention to detail. The good news is that pressing your pants does not necessarily mean dry cleaning them. You can press them with an iron in about a minute and bring your pants back to life. Before you do, however, make sure to check the material of your suit to be sure it can be ironed.

Line up the seams of your pants as detailed above, lay them on an ironing table, and press out the wrinkles. Depending on the fabric, consider using a pressing cloth or turning the pants inside out to avoid burning or a shiny surface to your pants. Either will look extremely unprofessional.

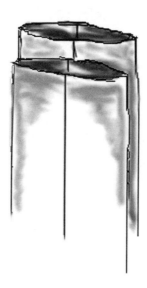

THE "GIG-LINE"

As you get ready to buckle your belt, look at your shirt. Your "Gig-Line" should be straight. The gig-line is a vertical line that runs the length of your body from your zipper to your collar. This line has three major components: pants, belt and shirt. The right side of your zipper should be even with the button on the top of your pants. Use this as your guide. Next, take the button line of your shirt and pull it down so that the right edge of the line is even with your zipper line. The third part requires you to pull the belt so that the right edge of your buckle is even with your pant and shirt line. Your tie will follow the gig-line naturally and end up at the bottom of your belt buckle. This is a straight gig-line, and it really makes a difference in overall professional appearance.

Gig-Line

JACKETS

The key to finding the right jacket is to buy a high quality suit that fits your frame, is well tailored, and is a basic color. Although some businessmen remove their suit jackets during the day, the jacket is an integral part of the professional wardrobe. Make sure to hang up your jacket when you are not wearing it, especially when you are driving to work. While sitting at your desk, remove your jacket if you can. Make sure you keep extra hangers in your office. When you wear your jacket, button only the top button. Walking with an open jacket looks sloppy, and buttoning two buttons looks too rigid. When you sit down while wearing a jacket, be sure to unbutton it. If you are interested in a classy look, consider a pocket handkerchief that matches your tie.

A suit that fits properly is the most fundamental aspect of professional attire. It is, however, not cheap. Again, as with all clothing, paying for quality is the best way to go. First, find the style of suit best fitted for your frame. There are three main styles: athletic, regular and full. If you have a typical American male frame, you will probably wear a regular style suit. If you are in great shape, the athletic style may be the best. If you have a more portly figure, try the full cut.

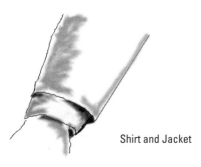

Shirt and Jacket

To find the right sleeve length, stretch your arms out in front of you. The edge of the sleeve should touch the wrist bone that sticks up on the outside of your arm. Fitting the shirt should be a similar process. The shirt should extend a half inch beyond the edge of the jacket when your arms are outstretched. To get the right jacket length, stand with your hands straight down, and your fingers curled as if to hold a pencil. The jacket bottom should just touch your fingers where the pencil would sit.

Buy the highest quality suit that looks good on you and that you can afford. Single breasted suits are considered slightly more professional and classier than double-breasted suits, but feel free to go with the look you prefer. The basic colors are navy blue and charcoal gray. Olive green and light gray are also acceptable in some professions.

Once you have purchased the right suit, you must prepare it before you wear it. Go to a qualified tailor and have your suits altered to fit your body. When your suit is back from the tailor, search for small pieces of loose thread improperly cut in the factory or by the tailor. These little strings are sometimes euphemistically referred to as "pendants." Good hiding places for the threads are near buttons, button holes, and on and near seams. Clip the threads as close to the body of the fabric as possible.

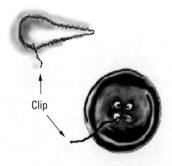

Clip

Cleaning Your Clothes

Stains and spots on your clothes are fact of life. What follows is a general guide on what you can use to remove certain spots. Aside from being quite annoying, paper cuts can go undetected until blood appears on your shirt. As soon as you notice a blood stain, blot it with a paper towel. Then run the fabric under cold water for a few minutes. At the earliest possible convenience, wash the fabric with color safe bleach.

Deodorant stains should be blotted with white vinegar, then the fabric washed with a color safe bleach in the hottest water allowable (check the label for the recommended temperature). An old perspiration stain that has caused the fabric to yellow should also be blotted with white vinegar. Fresh perspiration stains may be blotted with ammonia water (one teaspoon per quart). After blotting, soak the fabric in cold water, then wash it in the hottest water allowable for the fabric.

During the working day, other stains can occur. In general, most stains can be cleaned by blotting — not rubbing — then soaking the fabric under cold water. When you wash your clothes, use color-safe bleach. Coffee can be treated in this manner, as can chocolate, fruit juices and soft drinks. Ink from a ball-point pen can be removed from fabric with hair-spray. Simply spray the spot, let it soak into the fabric, then wash the garment with color-safe bleach.

In caring for your clothes, again, you must be willing to pay the price necessary to keep your appearance impeccable. If you tend to be thrifty, you might want to wear your shirts two or three times before getting them cleaned. Don't do it. Pay the extra money to wear a clean shirt every day. Wrinkles and spots will not only destroy your appearance, but your credibility as a professional as well.

On the other hand, there is no set rule for how often you must clean your suits. The Neighborhood Cleaning Association (an action group of Dry Cleaners) suggests cleaning after one to three wearings. Others say you can wait up to twelve wearings. As a general rule, you can wear your suits until you feel they are dirty and need to be cleaned. This usually means about five to ten wearings, but make sure you feel comfortable with the cleanliness of your wardrobe. When you dry clean your suits, have the pants and jacket done together to ensure that the color continues to match.

ACCESSORIES

Now that your clothes are set, you need accessories. For starters, you need a business watch. This is a watch that looks professional with your suits, but is not too flashy. As a general rule, leather and metal bands (gold, silver, stainless steel) are advisable. Avoid digital faces and plastic bands. Another important accessory is a leather belt. You will need one black belt and one brown belt, or a single convertible belt, with a nice silver or gold buckle. Remember, though, that you are not a cowboy, so keep the buckle size small.

Many professionals look great wearing braces, also called suspenders. Suspenders are a substitute for a belt, so wear one or the other, but not both. The key to wearing suspenders properly is to pay to have buttons sewn into your pants to anchor the straps. No self respecting professional (or even clown) wears clip-on suspenders. The color of your suspenders should match your tie. As usual, choosing a solid color or basic pattern makes matching much easier. Also remember that outlandish colors may not be appropriate.

Buy a high-quality pen and avoid carrying a cheap pen during any interview or meeting. You can find a nice pen for about $10, but don't be afraid to pay for quality. A prestigious pen will really make you look good, just as a cheap pen can take away from your professional appearance. Along with the pen, it is advisable to carry a leather-bound portfolio for important documents and your business cards. You can buy a generic portfolio, or carry one from your school or company. The idea is to carry loose papers in a professional-looking way at all times.

Cologne should be used sparingly since people are turned off by an overpowering scent. As a general rule, use about half the amount you would use if you were going on a date. Use it to enhance your appearance, not dominate it. Finally, assuming you do not have a beard or mustache, you must shave every day. There are no exceptions. An unshaven look will not give you the professional look you desire, no matter how well you dress.

To always look your best, consider keeping an extra dress shirt, tie and umbrella in your office or car. At some point, a stain on your shirt or tie is inevitable. Having an extra shirt and tie handy will add a level of security to your professional appearance. The extra umbrella will keep your suit dry, since a hard rain can really ruin a suit. Also, keep a few toothpicks in your car and briefcase. Nothing can be as embarrassing as noticing that you have part of your last meal in your teeth.

Be very careful about wearing any jewelry besides a watch. Wedding rings, and in some cases, college and military rings are also acceptable. Bracelets, necklaces and some rings, however, are not. Earrings, nose rings, eyebrow rings, and other rings in a pierced body part are generally taboo. Excessive jewelry is considered inappropriate. Now that the 1970s are well behind us, necklaces and bracelets in the workplace are, too. Tattoos are usually not acceptable in a professional environment. If you have one, keep it covered.

Another accessory is a lint roller, which is a rod with a cylinder of double sided tape on the end of it. You roll it over your clothes to pick up small pieces of lint, dirt, hair and other undesirable debris. If you have pets, you must use a lint roller. It can be a great tool, and because it is so cheap, you can keep several around for your convenience.

SEWING ON BUTTONS

Another key to maintaining your wardrobe is a rudimentary knowledge of sewing. This doesn't mean you have to make your own clothes, but having the ability to sew a button back on your shirt is important. You will need a needle, about two feet of thread and a button. You can buy these supplies cheaply at almost any store.

Begin by threading the needle such that you hold the two ends with one hand, and the needle one foot away from the other. Take the two loose ends and tie a triple knot. Now take the button and place it where the old button had been; there should be an indentation on the fabric.

Begin underneath the button side of the fabric, and push the needle through the fabric and into hole "A" (see below). Pull the needle through the hole until the knot is

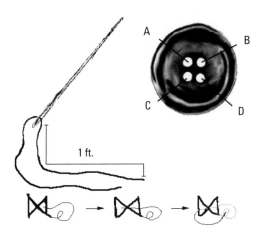

pulled tightly against the underside of the fabric. Each time you pull the needle through a hole and fabric, be sure to pull it completely through to eliminate any slack in the thread. Now put the needle through hole "B" into the fabric. From the underside, pull the needle through the fabric and into hole "D." Next, place the needle into hole "C" and through the fabric, remembering to pull it taut. This will hold the button in place and allow you to secure it for the actual sewing.

Now you can pull the needle through the fabric into hole "A," into hole "B," and back into the fabric. Return to hole "A" and repeat the process four times. After the fourth time through hole "B," pull the needle through the fabric and into hole "D." Pull the needle through hole "C," into the fabric, and back through hole "D." Repeat this four times.

Now that you're on the underside of the fabric, you'll need to tie off the end. To do this, pull the needle underneath the developed knot, and also a stitch or two of fabric. As you pull it through, leave a small loop at the old side. Pull the needle through the loop and pull the thread taut. Repeat this with another loop. Now, simply cut the thread just above the knot. With your button in place, you will easily maintain your wardrobe, saving you countless trips to the tailor.

MIXING AND MATCHING

Matching is a difficult prospect for most men. The key, for most men, is to stick to the basics unless you have great style. This is a rudimentary guide for those of you whose inability to match may severely limit your success.

The key element to a simple matching wardrobe is a white shirt, so begin with about eight. They are easiest to match with a tie and suit. Next, buy at least one charcoal gray and one navy blue suit and two pairs of black shoes. The keys to your simple wardrobe — and to disguising the fact that it is a simple wardrobe — are ties. You need about ten ties, in basic designs, such as paisley, solids, simple stripes, and small patterns. Red, maroon, and yellow ties are considered power colors, and go with both suit colors. Dark blue, royal blue, and green ties go well with gray, but not with navy. Black socks are the best bet, especially if you are wearing black shoes. Never wear socks that are darker than your shoes. If you wish, you can match your socks to the dark colors in your tie. Your socks (and pants) should be long enough so that when you cross your legs, no skin shows.

Building your wardrobe to a slightly more advanced level is not difficult. Try a gray suit with black shoes, a solid blue shirt and yellow tie. Another good combination is an olive suit with maroon (cordovan) shoes, white shirt and a multicolored tie with some olive in it. You may also consider a light gray suit, white shirt, red tie, and black shoes. These combinations will add some spice to your appearance while still remaining professional.

"BUSINESS CASUAL"

Almost everyone loves casual Fridays, but what does "casual" really mean in the workplace? Unfortunately, there is no universal definition. As a general guide, if you are at all unsure about how casual you can be, do not guess. Wear appropriate professional clothing on the first casual day and observe what your co-workers wear. Depending on your type of business, the weather, your city, and the standards of casual dressing in your office, what is considered casual may vary greatly.

Khakis or dark dress pants are generally acceptable everywhere. With a collared, buttoned down shirt, you can fit into almost any casual workplace. When weather permits, a golf or polo shirt may be acceptable; jeans often are not, so check with your co-workers before you risk it. Hats are never appropriate, nor are T-shirts or shorts. You can wear boat shoes, loafers, or even your usual dress shoes if they match the rest of your clothes. In the winter, a sweater is a good idea. Be sure to wear a collared shirt underneath it. Remember, you do have co-workers, so do not forget socks.

Clothes Checklist

Here is a summary of the clothes you should have in your professional wardrobe:

Clothes	Quantity	Description
Suits	2-6	At least one charcoal gray and navy blue to start
Dress Shirts	12+	Broken down as follows
White	8	
Solid Color	2	Blue and Pink
Striped	2	Blue with White and Maroon with White
Ties	10	Conservative, not "fun" ties
Dress Shoes	2-3	Black and Brown
Dress Belts	2	One black and one brown or a single convertible
Socks	18	
Raincoat	1	
Accessories		
Watch	1	High quality
Umbrellas	2	One in the car, one in the office
Quality Pen	1	

If you have these items, you will dress like a professional gentleman. Remember, high-quality clothes and accessories will help you look great with much less effort.

PHYSICAL FITNESS

A discussion of professional appearance would be incomplete without at least mentioning the benefits of staying, or getting, in shape. Although there are successful professionals who succeed without being in shape, many truly successful businessmen are in great shape. They spend the time to work-out and tone their bodies to get in shape. They also have more stamina and are able to more easily deal with working late hours. It is easier to fit into your clothes, you will have more energy, and you will look like a mover and shaker.

This does not mean that your career depends on four hours a day in the gym. By taking about one hour every other day, you can trim down, keep your heart in shape, and have more energy. After consulting with your doctor, establish a work-out plan. Decide the time of day you will work out and what you will do. Allow about an hour for your workout, plus time to cool down and for a shower afterwards. If you do this every other day for a month, you will see a positive change in your professional appearance.

After you work-out, make sure to take care of your body by drinking water. A gallon of water a day is recommended. This may sound like a lot, but water is the most important component of your body. Refresh it, and you will stay healthy and in shape. Instead of eating three meals a day, try eating only when you are hungry, even if that means six or seven times a day. Eat just until you are no longer hungry, not until you are full. This will raise your metabolism, allowing you to burn fat at a more rapid rate.

Posture

Good posture is an important part of your appearance. The way you sit, stand and walk are all interpreted by others as keys to your attitude, strength and ability to accomplish difficult tasks. "Go-getters" sit up straight, stand with style, and walk tall. So, how should you carry yourself?

When sitting down, sit as if you have a string attached to your chest. Imagine that the string is pulling you up, so that you sit up straight. This will allow you to think more clearly, feel more energetic, and look professional. When standing, fight the urge to put your hands in your pockets, fold your arms, or move your hands. If you are constantly fidgeting, you will attract attention away from your words. The most professional way to stand when waiting or speaking with someone is with your hands at your sides in a relaxed position. This conveys your willingness to listen, your patience and professionalism. You can really take away from your own credibility by walking hunched over. When you are walking, imagine that the string that was attached to your chest is now moving with you, keeping your shoulders and head straight, and chin up. Smile when you walk, even if you live in New York. When you grimace, you appear angry; smiling also helps boost your attitude too.

CHIVALRY

Those who say chivalry is dead are wrong. Those who say chivalry is chauvinistic are also wrong. A true gentleman treats men and women alike with respect. When you get to a door first, hold it open for others before you enter yourself. After you have gone through it, look behind to see if you could hold it for someone else. When entering an elevator, wait for all people exiting to leave, then hold the door for anyone waiting. When you reach your floor, hold the door for anyone who wants to enter. When at a table, push in the chair in for any woman who needs assistance.

When you are walking down the street with some-one, take the position on the outside closest to the cars. This is considered old-fashioned, but extremely classy. Although the pragmatic need to stand on the outside is considerably lessened in this modern era of paved streets, any observant person will see the gentlemanly nature of your acts.

When you get to a car, open the door for women first, then you may enter. Remember that the most senior person should sit in the most comfortable seat, usually in the front. It is a good rule to be the last one in the car, especially if you are driving. The concepts of chivalry and gender equality are not mutually exclusive. A true gentleman knows that by being chivalrous, he is simply being kind and considerate, not asserting his dominance.

Business Etiquette

In the business world, proper etiquette is a must. Those who do not follow the rules of accepted behavior lose. Although this book is not long enough to discuss every aspect of proper etiquette, what follows is a rudimentary guide to selected important aspects.

Proper appearance is part of proper etiquette. The other major aspect is demeanor, or what you say and how you act in a professional setting. Obvious points include avoiding emotional topics (such as religion and politics), and using standard English when speaking (no slang, jargon or vernacular).

Also keep in mind that seemingly insignificant aspects like good posture and a calm smile give the appearance of strength and a positive attitude. While others may not consciously notice, studies show that people react more favorably to those with good posture and a smile. Notice that a calm smile is key, not a wide grin. A calm smile exudes dignity and power, and is proven to relax others around you. When walking with co-workers, be courteous. If you walk unusually slow or fast, adjust your speed to accommodate the others in your group. If you have a kitchen or coffee station in your office, do not be afraid to make coffee. Clean up after yourself. Spend an extra three minutes to clean up a mess or wash a dish or two, and you will generate an amazing amount of goodwill.

A business card is key to establishing yourself in the professional world. Hand them out to your friends, family, new and old acquaintances, and those who you feel may benefit you in the future. Also remember to ask for others' cards and save them; building a large file of cards can really pay off in the future. When you get a card, jot a few notes on the back about how you met the person, issues you discussed, and personal information that you have in common. Keep them in a centralized location like a planner or a special three ring binder with custom sheets that hold business cards. Contact the people at least once a year to keep the lines of communication open. Many people send a holiday card to everyone on their list; the minor marginal cost can help to build your professional image.

Shaking Hands

Although shaking hands takes only about three seconds, the reality of the gesture is that it forms a huge part of someone's initial impression of you. Even if you know people well, shaking their hand improperly diminishes your credibility as a professional. There are countless ways to shake hands improperly: you can offer a "dead fish," you can grab someone's fingers, you can squeeze too hard you can use two hands. Instead of describing every way not to do it, what follows is a description of the proper way to shake hands.

When the opportunity presents itself, square your shoulders to the person you want to greet. Smile, look them in the eye, and extend your right hand. Your fingers should be relatively close to each other, but not actually touching, and your thumb should be pointed straight up. As your hand meets the other hand, make sure you try to touch your thumb-finger web to that of the other person. Next, place your thumb on their hand, and squeeze it as if you were squeezing the ketchup out of a plastic container. You should shake for about three pumps, then slowly pull your hand away. Name tags should be worn on the right breast pocket to make it easier for others to read your name when you shake their hands. When you are standing at a cocktail party, be sure to keep your drink in your left hand. Since you will shake with your right hand, you do not want it to be cold and wet from the glass. If you shake someone's hand and find theirs to be wet, cold, or sweaty, do not draw attention to the condition, even in a joking manner. Act as if it were completely normal and move on. By politely ignoring it, you will help the other person feel accepted and consequently more comfortable with you.

As odd as it sounds, practice shaking hands with family members or friends. Your goal is to let the other person know that you have a strong handshake, but are not trying to break every bone in their hand. With a good handshake you will present a strong first impression, and again illustrate your attention to detail.

TABLE MANNERS

As this book reflects professional conduct, it would be incomplete without a discussion of table manners. Many professional meetings begin, include, or conclude with a meal. While good manners may not explicitly help you, bad manners will definitely hurt you.

To get your bearings, see the illustration of a typical table setting. The simplest rule for using silverware is a good one to follow, namely work from the outside in towards the plate. Your forks are on the left. If there are two, the smaller, outside fork is the salad fork, and the larger, inner one is, your dinner fork. On the right, from the outside, is your soup spoon, followed by your teaspoon, and knife with its blade facing towards the plate. Spoons and forks found above your plate are for desert, and your beverage the upper right corner of your table setting. Your salad plate is on your left side with your bread plate, and your coffee cup is on your right.

As soon as you sit down at the table, find the napkin, unfold it, and put it on your lap. Next, leave your non-dominant hand on your lap, and keep it there for most of the meal. You will want to eat with your dominant hand. The only time you will use both hands is to cut your food. To cut properly, hold your fork up-side down with your non-dominant hand, and your knife with your dominant hand. As soon as you have finished cutting, place the knife back on the right side of the plate or across the top of the plate, and switch your fork to your dominant hand to eat.

When eating bread, break off a small piece, butter it, and eat it. Do not butter the whole piece of bread or roll all at once. Also do not cut your food into many pieces. Simply cut off the piece you will eat, chew it well, and then cut again. Use your napkin often to clean any crumbs or food pieces from your lips.

When you finish with a spoon, place it on the saucer under your soup dish or coffee cup, not in the bowl. As soon as you have finished your meal, place your knife across the top of the plate, with the blade facing you. Next place your

fork and other used utensils closer to the middle of the plate, tines down, and parallel to the knife. As soon as you complete your meal, use your napkin, fold it loosely, and place it on the table. If you follow these simple rules, you will greatly lessen the chances of committing a serious faux pas at a business meal.

When sitting at a table with mixed company, it is a gentlemanly gesture to stand when a woman arrives or leaves the table. Also, when you are sitting and see someone you know, or are introduced to someone, rise to shake their hand. In this modern era, most people will say that standing is not necessary. When they do, you may stop rising, but in the meantime, you have shown to others your knowledge of good manners.

Writing A Resumé

A good resumé can help you land the job of your dreams. A bad resumé, however, can ensure that you will not get the job. What follows are some basic tips that can really help promote yourself through your resumé. The first, and most important thing, is to be honest. Aside from the obvious moral problems involved with lying, there are numerous other reasons to be honest. For those of you who might be tempted to lie or "embellish" your resumé, what follows is why you should not.

Interviewers and human resources (HR) professionals are, by their nature, detectives. Most examine every detail with a suspicious eye, and are trained to look for lies. Let's be clear: if you lie on your resumé and get caught (and you will eventually be caught), you will not get the job, or worse, will be subsequently fired after the truth is known. Plus, people will talk. When the word gets out that you are dishonest, your career is over. It is as simple as that.

However, it is important not to be modest. Your resumé is the best, and maybe the only chance to "toot your own horn." Tell prospective employers the good things you have done. If you have accomplished something special, talk about it. Unless you were the valedictorian, captain of the football team and national merit scholar, you may think you have nothing to say, but that is rarely true. Simply look back on the last few years and find the things you did that will make you marketable in the job market.

Set up a resumé in the following format. Begin with your full name, centered across the top. Use a font size slightly larger than that of the body of the resumé. If you have one address, center it below your name, and include your phone number and Email address as well. If you have two addresses — for example if you are in college and live away from home — list both, justifying each against the side columns. Again, include phone and Email addresses with both.

In discussing addresses and phone numbers, one word of caution must be included. Be careful using your current employer's address, phone or Email address on your resumé. Unless you are certain that your current employer will not mind that you are looking for a new job, use only your home address, phone and Email. Having said that, be sure you have an answering machine or voicemail at your home. Also, remember that your potential employer will hear your message, so be certain that it is professional, short, and to the point. Try something like "Hello. You have reached <first and last name>. I'm sorry I cannot take your call now, but if you would please leave your name and telephone number, I will return your call as soon as possible." Below your name, address, phone and Email at the top of the page, you should insert a line separating this information from the body of the resumé.

State your employment objective clearly and professionally. For example, "To obtain full time employment with a major public accounting firm." If your actual objective is unclear, or you do not feel comfortable including one, do not use one. Keep in mind that you may change objectives to conform to each job for which you are applying.

The education section of your resumé should come next. Depending on the last level completed, you may include or exclude high school data. (If you have your Ph.D., high school information will probably not interest your employers.) If you are a recent college graduate, you probably want to include your high school name, GPA, any honors received, sports played, and activities in which you were involved. Be smart. If you did well, say so. If you were not a star student, do not say anything. Build up your strengths, and avoid your weaknesses. To the far right of the information, include the years you were in school, as well as the location of each.

Experience or employment history usually comes next. Here you want to focus on your accomplishments, showing the jobs you have had, and how they relate to your objective, a perspective position, or your potential employer's business. The final section can include your hobbies, interest, and involvement in outside groups and organizations. Remember that it is up to you what you include on your resumé. If you feel that the inclusion or exclusion of any item is justified and will help a potential employer make a decision in your favor, go for it. Keep your resumé condensed and to the point. If you are new to the job world, try to keep it to just one page.

INTERVIEWING

When you obtain an appointment for an interview with a prospective employer, learn about the company and the job for which you are applying before the interview takes place. The Internet is a great place to start, but company newsletters, annual reports and magazine articles also can be helpful.

Try to gain a general understanding of the company as if you were going to write a report about it. Find out who the top officers are, and if possible, their personality types. Almost without exception, the leader's personality is indicative of the corporate culture. Also study current events involving the company and its industry. You can be sure that most topics in the news will be fair game for the interviewer's questions. Current events will also give you a good base for questions to ask.

Arrive to the interview a few minutes early, in your most professional attire. Once the interview starts, you will have a few moments to get the feel for the interviewer. Build rapport with him or her by sitting up straight, smiling softly, and looking him or her in the eyes when you speak. The first few minutes will create the interviewer's basic impression of you, and quite possibly, affect your chances of getting hired. Often he or she will begin the interview by discussing your resumé or an employment form designed by their company. Since the information will be familiar to you, this will help you relax. As discussed earlier in the resumé section, you must be honest. If you lie, you will be uncomfortable and stressed during the interview instead of being relaxed and freely discussing your accomplishments. Be modest, but positive about your experiences and be sure to be able to explain how you overcame problems or hurdles in your life. Most interviewers now ask you for a situation in which you dealt with difficulty or failure, and what you learned in the process. If you were previously employed, the interviewer will almost always ask about your former employer. Do not take this as an invitation to complain about how horrible your experience was, or how much you hate your old boss, even if it is true. This question is designed to evaluate what kind of relationship you had with your previous employer. Be sure to be honest, but do not say that your boss hated you, or you hated him or her. Try to mention the benefits of working at that job, and what you learned there that will help you in your next position.

At the end of every interview, you will be given an opportunity to ask questions. Use it. Find out what you want to know, but have not been able to learn from your initial research. Having said that, there is such a thing as a stupid question in an interview situation. This can include asking how much money the position pays, the vacation policy, what does the company do, and what are your chances of getting the job. Make a point to ask something that will help you to be chosen above other candidates. Ask about a "day in the life" of the person currently in the position for which you are applying, or how the company can offer you growth, both personally and professionally. Depending on the interviewer's perceived receptivity for suggestions, you might want to use your earlier research on the company to make a suggestion for a new opportunity they might consider. Many companies would appreciate this initiative.

After the interview, be sure to follow up with a written thank-you letter to the interviewer or interviewers. This can take the form of a card or letter. The most important part is to thank the individual for their time and effort. You may also answer questions you were unable to answer during the interview, provide other information, or ask another question. Be sure to personalize the communication by making a reference to your interview. If you meet with more than one person, be sure to send separate thank you letters to each.

Being On Time And Organized

Not everyone finds being on time easy. Most people who arrive on time and call when they say they will, have to work at it. Professionals must become masters of time. Making a point of being exactly on time is an obvious way of showing your attention to detail. People who are known for punctuality are also well respected and trusted.

When arriving for a meeting, show up about one minute before the scheduled time of the meeting. You do not want to rush someone by showing up well before your set time. On the other hand, being late shows a lack of consideration. If you become unavoidably detained, call. That is what cellular or digital phones are for. Realize, however, that you should make every effort to be on time. The first time you plan to meet someone at an unfamiliar location — or if you are concerned about being late — plan on arriving 15 to 20 minutes early. You can use this extra time in your car or outside the building to deal with small administrative tasks.

The key to good organization is planning, so get a good planner. Many different styles are available, and as long as you will use it, the type does not matter. First, make sure that it allows you to plan on a daily, weekly, monthly, and long-term basis. It should also have room for names, addresses, and phone numbers. Some even have clear plastic sheets that can hold about six business cards per page. Keep the cards you use most in these pages. For the others that you accumulate, you should consider getting a three ring-binder with ten card sheets as previously mentioned. This will allow you to keep them in an accessible, portable form.

BUSINESS COMMUNICATION

A business letter is an important part of professional communication. By following the proper format, you will illustrate to the reader your knowledge of business culture and how to act with attention to detail. It is best if you justify all type on the left. Begin your letter with the date, followed by the name and address of the individual to whom you are writing. Next, greet the reader by the name you commonly use in conversation. If you have not met, do not use their first name. Make the letter as clear, straightforward and easy to read as possible. In the first or second sentence, convey the purpose of writing, and spend the rest of the letter discussing the point. Do your best to keep the letter to one page. Single space the type but include an extra space between paragraphs. You may or may not indent the first line of each paragraph: it is a matter of personal style. When you complete the body of the text, conclude with "Sincerely," or "Best regards." Leave a few spaces for your signature, then type your full name below.

The proper format for a business memo is constantly changing, but the following is a basic template. First, type a capitalized "MEMORANDUM" to signify the format. Next, justify all type on the left, and begin with the date, then skip a few lines, and identify the recipient by his or her complete name preceded by a "To:". Next, after a "From:," type your full name. Below the names, type "Re:" or "Subj.:" and then indicate the reason for your communication. This should be three or four words describing the memo. Then write your paragraphs as separate groups, without indenting the first line. No conclusion is necessary. After you have printed it out, initial it to the right of your name.

Email and voicemail are growing in popularity since most offices use both as communicating tools. Although these formats are informal forms of communication, remember that you are a professional, and need to conduct yourself as one. Begin your Emails with the proper salutation, use professional language, and keep it short. In a voicemail, greet the person, convey your point clearly, and keep the message short. Most voicemail systems allow you to erase and re-record your messages if you make a mistake. Take advantage of this option; you always want to sound the best you can. This may mean taking extra time to learn the system, and the functions it performs.

EMAIL PRIVACY

Email is now a common form of communication in most workplaces. Many employees connect to the Internet and communicate with friends and family all over the world on company time. Some employers condone this, others do not. Be sure to check your company's policy on personal Emails during working hours before unnecessarily endangering your job. The problem arises when employees believe that the messages they send are private. By law, every Email you send and receive at work can be read by your employer. It is unclear how many companies check messages, but the important point is that the possibility exists. When using Email at work assume that your boss and everyone else will read every word you write.

If you feel the need to send personal Emails, establish a personal account through an Internet Service Provider. There are also several free Email services on the Internet. Realize that the same laws exist for surfing the Internet and visiting the web. Any employer can get a listing of every web site you visited when using your employer's system, so be careful. If you do visit sites that you would not want the entire office to know about, surf the net away from work. Also, be sparing in your non-business use of the Internet. Your employer can track the time you spend and locations you visit on the web, and this could definitely be a career-limiting move.

OFFICE POLITICS

"People will talk." You have heard it before, but now at work, it is much more prevalent. When you finally get your job, you will find office politics and the proverbial "grapevine" not only exist, but often run rampant. You must be prepared for this; expect it and accept it. Unfortunately, it is human nature.

Having said this, do not play the game. It is very easy to sit with your co-workers and complain about your boss, other co-workers, or subordinates. Do not do it. There are no good reasons to sit in on these discussions, let alone participate in them. The information — or misinformation — is harmful not only to the subjects of the discussion, but to the speaker and the listener as well. By participating, you often gather faulty information. Think about it. If you tell others how you dislike someone with whom you are usually pleasant, they will realize that they cannot trust anything you say. Rise above gossip. Stick to your work and the tasks that will help you succeed. You will be stronger for it in the end.

Conclusion

With the simple techniques discussed in this book, you can begin to take command of your appearance and professional demeanor. People will notice your attention to detail, and understand that you care about your appearance and professional reputation. If you keep your appearance in order and act like a gentleman, you will probably find that you are treated with respect. But most importantly, you will also feel more comfortable about yourself, and be able to do your best work. Remember, attention to detail can be a great help to your career, and your life.

If you have any thoughts, ideas, suggestions, questions or comments, please send them to: Clint Greenleaf, Greenleaf Enterprises, P.O. Box 291, Chesterland, Ohio 44026. You can also send an Email to: ctg3@hotmail.com or call 212-330-1458

THE PRODUCTS OF
GREENLEAF ENTERPRISES

The Attention to Detail Newsletter

The Attention to Detail Newsletter is now in print! As a preferred customer, you are eligible for the discounted price of only $19.95 for a full year subscription. The newsletter provides a monthly review of topics discussed in this book, as well as financial and cooking subjects. The newsletter expands the advice and guidance to include seasonal trends and new developments in the professional world.

Additional Copies of this Book

For our customers, we offer an option to purchase additional copies of this book free of shipping costs. This book makes a great gift for any young gentleman and is available for only $12.95 per book.

Bulk Orders

If you are business or not-for-profit institution, and are interested in a bulk purchase, please forward your request, including the quantity and product you would like to purchase.

Speaking Engagements

Clint Greenleaf may be available for speaking engagements for your group or company. An accomplished public speaker, Clint has presented this topic to several different groups and large companies. If you are interested in discussing the options for a presentation, or would like a list of references, please send a proposal to Greenleaf Enterprises.

For any of these products see the Order Form on the next page.

ORDER FORM

☐ **The Attention to Detail Newsletter**

   $19.95 each x _____ subscriptions = $ _____

☐ **Additional Copies of this Book**

   $12.95 each x _____ copies = $ _____

Please send information on:

☐ **Bulk Orders**   ☐ **Speaking Engagements**

Make check or money order payable to Greenleaf Enterprises with the applicable sales tax. Send this order form and your payment to: Greenleaf Enterprises, Preferred Customer Department, P.O. Box 291, Chesterland, Ohio 44026.

Name _____

Address _____

City _____

State _____ *Zip Code* _____

Phone _____

Email _____

NOTES

Notes

NOTES